Revealed
BIBLE STUDY METHOD

The Letters of Galatians and Ephesians

Jenn Avey

Copyright © 2020 by Jenn Avey

All rights reserved. No part of this publication may be reproduced or used in any manner without the written permission of the copyright owner.

World English Bible (WEB) public domain usage.

Acknowledgements

I'm still a student and have lots to learn. The following people have been pivotal in teaching me, each with a unique hand in seeing this method solidify to the journal you now hold.

My husband, Scott, is always my biggest fan. His support, and I don't just mean for this project, keeps me trying new things and embracing the journey. My parents and in-laws are consistent sources of encouragement and helpful feedback. My dearest friend, Lorena, is a loyal companion who inspires my soul to depend on Jesus and trust Him completely.

Tabby helped me make sense out of my original mind dumps. Josie helped me brainstorm and reform ideas. Amanda graciously coached me as I talked myself in circles trying to navigate next steps. Ashley with Well Versed Design, took content and made it printable, practical, and beautiful.

What God's Spirit accomplishes through all of us, you included, as we work together to advance Christ's Kingdom is beyond an acknowledgement. Whatever passion is in your heart today, work as unto the Lord and offer it as a sacrifice of praise. This journal is a collective act of worship to our Creator and Savior.

From the Author

My dearest friend is an artist. Her studio is full of works in progress. Many times I've commented on a piece only to hear, "That's just the under-painting." Her art requires layers of color and texture and each trip to the easel adds something to be uncovered when studying the canvas. The more I study my friend's art, the more I learn about her. Understanding the art helps me understand the artist. The Holy Scriptures are also a unique masterpiece that displays artist and artwork. Understanding God's written revelation is essential to understanding God. The art reveals the Artist.

As a young believer, I studied my Bible, but alternative beliefs and arguments confronted my child-like faith in college. I needed a better understanding of God's Word and God Himself. For the last 20 years, I have used numerous Bible study methods, but it wasn't until I began to process my study through the principals of sound interpretation that the artistry of Scripture came to LIFE.

I wrote this study method as a student-teacher for the benefit of other students and teachers. As a curious and committed Bible **student**, I desired an accessible and sound study method. As a small group **leader**, I wanted to understand the text well before leading the discussion. As a responsible Bible **teacher**, I sought to instruct from a solid method that fosters interpretation AND application. That is why I created the Revealed Journal. I wanted to provide a Bible study method that engages with and appreciates the layers of the text. This unique study method is a hermeneutically sound tool that guides us to see that there is more to be revealed if we look beyond the surface and linger a little longer. My prayer is that this method gives you the confidence to dive into the difficult questions, find the beauty in the artwork and the Artist, and through the process, know the God who is Revealed.

Jenn Avey

P.S. I'd love to connect with you online! Follow me on Facebook, Instagram, and get study aids and helps on my YouTube channel.
facebook.com/jenn.avey
instagram.com/jenn_avey/
youtube.com/c/JennAvey

Table of Contents

The Letters

Galatians

- Prepare 16-17
- Divide, World English Bible Translation 18-22
- Journal Instructions and Pages 28-57
- Revealed Truths 106

Ephesians

- Prepare 62-63
- Divide, World English Bible Translation 64-73
- Journal Instructions and Pages 74-105
- Revealed Truths 108

Resources

- Resources 110-111
- Genre Guide 112-113
- Divide Sample 114
- Journal Bookmarks 115

The Method

The Revealed Bible Study Method is a guide to help us understand what God has revealed in Scripture. Our God has chosen to reveal Himself through the act of creating and interacting with His creation. He has chosen both general and special ways of unveiling who He is and what He is doing. All nature, the earth, skies, and heavens display His character (Rom 1:19-20, Ps. 19:1-5). But He also selected certain men to record and pass on special acts of God's self-disclosure (2 Pet. 1:20-21). These men were inspired, led by the Holy Spirit God, to write as they were directed (2 Tim. 3:16). They wrote in normal modes of communication and followed standard writing practices and methods of their day. These ancient authors lived long ago and far away. They wrote from various backgrounds, covering works from histrory, law, poetry, and even personal correspondence. The diversity of authorship and content is staggering, but the consistency and singularity of their purpose is even more awe-inspiring. They were human authors, writing to human audiences, carried along by God's Spirit to reveal God Himself. Every word, every story, every poem, revealing a real time and place in ancient history past AND truths that transcend that people and place. It is this very important aspect of the Bible's dual nature, both human and divine, that makes understanding and application challenging at times.

Using principles for solid biblical interpretation alongside inductive Bible study methods, Revealed focuses on the unique human and divine nature of each of the 66 books in the Holy Bible. What was written back *then to them* is also *for us now*. The acronyms and processes we use in this method will help us focus on both- them and then, us and now.

L I F E is the acronym the Revealed method uses for the principles of the historical-grammatical biblical hermeneutic. Those are just fancy words that mean we understand the Bible when we place the written texts within their proper contexts. L I F E walks us through 4 of those critical contexts- historical, grammatical, literary, and biblical. But just knowing the text does not necessarily change our lives. We must decide what we are going to DO with our understanding. The acronym L I V E offers application principles to help us do just that, to live now in light of God's revelation. Alongside both of these acronyms, we will observe, summarize, and outline in order to allow the text to speak for itself. Each step in our process aims to bring us closer to what God has revealed in the Scriptures.

It's a METHOD! The Revealed Bible Study Method may be unlike anything you've done before. Before you begin, I suggest you get familiar with the method instructions for each step. The instructions are directly before each section of the journal, so flip to the Prepare (pg16), Divide (pg18), and Journal (pg28) sections and READ the directions first. Trust me! Don't expect to master everything right away. As you work through the process, you'll see more and more revealed. It will take time, intention, and energy, but I assure you, it will reap lasting rewards. You'll never study Scripture the same way again! Join me as we look deeply within Scripture, deeply within ourselves, and gaze upon the beauty of God's revelation.

Revealed Bible Study

Prepare

Build a solid foundation for interpretation by reading or listening to the entire book and answering the initial context questions.

Divide

Go deeper into the book by dividing it into sections for further study. These blocks of Scripture will provide manageable pieces for deeper examination.

Journal

Work through your in-depth study using the Revealed Journal. Take each passage section and summarize, observe, and outline.

Take time with each passage to find L I F E and L I V E!

Gather your Revealed Truths together in the back of your journal.

Galatians

Prepare: Galatians

Gather Context

The first step to studying any passage of Scripture is gathering context. For each book you will study, understanding the larger context is essential to sound interpretation. The best way to gather context is by **reading the whole book**! You can read or listen to the audio book in your favorite version. The purpose is to see the broader story from beginning to end before digging beneath the surface. Refer to a few outside resources to answer the initial context questions below in the boxes on the next page.

- Who is the author(s) and audience?
- What do you know about them?
- Where is the author and audience?
- What are the key features of their location?
- When was this book written?
- When did the events in the book take place?
- When did the events take place in terms of redemptive history? Flood, Exodus, Exile, church age, etc
- What is the main genre of this book? Narrative, law, poetry, etc.
- What are the key literary features of this book?

Pray for Wisdom

You won't notice prayer as a separate step listed in this method. Prayer isn't a piece of the process, it permeates the process. Prayer is a two-way conversation with God: honest sharing and reflective listening. God doesn't begin to listen to us at 'Dear Heavenly Father' and shut off at 'Amen'. We want to acknowledge His presence always. Throughout the whole process we are praying and asking for wisdom and understanding. Start to finish, we revel in conversation with the One revealing Himself to us.

Who

Where

When

Genre

Divide

Instructions

For each book in this journal, you will find a copy of the World English Bible (WEB) translation with all chapter and verse marks removed. Why? Because **you** will do the work of dividing the passage into sections for yourself! The goal is to break each book into smaller sections to study in your Revealed Journal.

The chapter and verse markings in your Bible are not inspired and are placed there to make passages easier to read and reference. Sub-headings are the translator's attempt at dividing up longer passages into smaller stories or main ideas, but these are not original to the biblical texts. Reading Scripture with these markings removed allows us to find the main ideas for ourselves. It gives us as modern readers a good starting point for reading the text as the original audience would have received it.

So turn to the book you are studying, grab a pencil, and start placing brackets in the margin where you think a main idea starts and stops. Look for clues in the text that indicate a change in subject, location, tone, etc. **Group together verses and paragraphs that cover one big idea, singular event, or key theological concept.** Once you have a few pages marked, grab the Bible translation you plan to use for your study and compare your bracketed sections. Write the corresponding chapter and verse numbers along your bracketed margin. These sections will be the Revealed Passages you work through in your journal. Reference the sample in the back if needed. With larger books, its best to divide a few pages and then start journaling. Galatians is a smaller book, so try and divide the whole book before beginning your journaling.

The WEB copy in your journal also gives you the opportunity to mark up your observations on your subsequent readings. Use different colored pens to circle key words, underline main ideas, or highlight questions. Some people are more hesitant to mark up their actual Bible, but feel free to mark up this copy however you like!

Galatians

Paul, an apostle—not from men, nor through man, but through Jesus Christ, and God the Father, who raised him from the dead— and all the brothers who are with me, to the assemblies of Galatia: Grace to you and peace from God the Father and our Lord Jesus Christ, who gave himself for our sins, that he might deliver us out of this present evil age, according to the will of our God and Father— to whom be the glory forever and ever. Amen.

I marvel that you are so quickly deserting him who called you in the grace of Christ to a different "good news", but there isn't another "good news." Only there are some who trouble you and want to pervert the Good News of Christ. But even though we, or an angel from heaven, should preach to you any "good news" other than that which we preached to you, let him be cursed. As we have said before, so I now say again: if any man preaches to you any "good news" other than that which you received, let him be cursed. For am I now seeking the favor of men, or of God? Or am I striving to please men? For if I were still pleasing men, I wouldn't be a servant of Christ. But I make known to you, brothers, concerning the Good News which was preached by me, that it is not according to man. For I didn't receive it from man, nor was I taught it, but it came to me through revelation of Jesus Christ. For you have heard of my way of living in time past in the Jews' religion, how that beyond measure I persecuted the assembly of God and ravaged it. I advanced in the Jews' religion beyond many of my own age among my countrymen, being more exceedingly zealous for the traditions of my fathers. But when it was the good pleasure of God, who separated me from my mother's womb and called me through his grace to reveal his Son in me, that I might preach him among the Gentiles, I didn't immediately confer with flesh and blood, nor did I go up to Jerusalem to those who were apostles before me, but I went away into Arabia. Then I returned to Damascus.

Then after three years I went up to Jerusalem to visit Peter, and stayed with him fifteen days. But of the other apostles I saw no one except James, the Lord's brother. Now about the things which I write to you, behold, before God, I'm not lying. Then I came to the regions of Syria and Cilicia. I was still unknown by face to the assemblies of Judea which were in Christ, but they only heard: "He who once persecuted us now preaches the faith that he once tried to destroy." So they glorified God in me.

Then after a period of fourteen years I went up again to Jerusalem with Barnabas, taking Titus also with me. I went up by revelation, and I laid before them the Good News which I preach among the Gentiles, but privately before those who were respected, for fear that I might be running, or had run, in vain. But not even Titus, who was with me, being a Greek, was compelled to be circumcised. This was because of the false brothers secretly brought in, who stole in to spy out our liberty which we have in Christ Jesus, that they might bring us into bondage, to whom we gave no place in the way of subjection, not for an hour, that the truth of the Good News might continue with you. But from those who were reputed to be important—whatever they were, it makes no difference to me; God doesn't show partiality to man—they, I say, who were respected imparted nothing to me, but to the contrary, when they saw that I had been entrusted with the Good News for the uncircumcised, even as Peter with the Good News for the circumcised— for he who worked through Peter in the apostleship with the circumcised also worked through me with the Gentiles— and when they perceived the grace that was given to me, James and Cephas and John, those who were reputed to be pillars, gave to Barnabas and me the right hand of fellowship, that we should go to the Gentiles, and they to the circumcision. They only asked us to remember the poor—which very thing I was also zealous to do.

But when Peter came to Antioch, I resisted him to his face, because he stood condemned. For before some people came from James, he ate with the Gentiles. But when they came, he drew back and separated himself, fearing those who were of the circumcision. And the rest of the Jews joined him in his hypocrisy, so that even Barnabas was carried away with their hypocrisy. But when I saw that they didn't walk uprightly according to the truth of the Good News, I said to Peter before them all, "If you, being a Jew, live as the Gentiles do, and not as the Jews do, why do you compel the Gentiles to live as the Jews do?

"We, being Jews by nature, and not Gentile sinners, yet knowing that a man is not justified by the works of the law but through faith in Jesus Christ, even we believed in Christ Jesus, that we might be justified by faith in Christ, and not by the works of the law, because no flesh will be justified by the works of the law. But if while we sought to be justified in Christ, we ourselves also were found sinners, is Christ a servant of sin? Certainly not! For if I build up again those things which I destroyed, I prove myself a law-breaker. For I, through the law, died to the law, that I might live to God. I have been crucified with Christ, and it is no longer I who live, but Christ lives in me. That life which I now live in the flesh, I live by faith in the Son of God, who loved me, and gave himself up for me. I don't reject the grace of God. For if righteousness is through the law, then Christ died for nothing!"

Foolish Galatians, who has bewitched you not to obey the truth, before whose eyes Jesus Christ was openly portrayed among you as crucified? I just want to learn this from you: Did you receive the Spirit by the works of the law, or by hearing of faith? Are you so foolish? Having begun in the

Spirit, are you now completed in the flesh? Did you suffer so many things in vain, if it is indeed in vain? He therefore who supplies the Spirit to you and does miracles among you, does he do it by the works of the law, or by hearing of faith? Even so, Abraham "believed God, and it was counted to him for righteousness." Know therefore that those who are of faith are children of Abraham. The Scripture, foreseeing that God would justify the Gentiles by faith, preached the Good News beforehand to Abraham, saying, "In you all the nations will be blessed." So then, those who are of faith are blessed with the faithful Abraham. For as many as are of the works of the law are under a curse. For it is written, "Cursed is everyone who doesn't continue in all things that are written in the book of the law, to do them." Now that no man is justified by the law before God is evident, for, "The righteous will live by faith." The law is not of faith, but, "The man who does them will live by them."

Christ redeemed us from the curse of the law, having become a curse for us. For it is written, "Cursed is everyone who hangs on a tree," that the blessing of Abraham might come on the Gentiles through Christ Jesus, that we might receive the promise of the Spirit through faith. Brothers, speaking of human terms, though it is only a man's covenant, yet when it has been confirmed, no one makes it void or adds to it. Now the promises were spoken to Abraham and to his offspring. He doesn't say, "To descendants", as of many, but as of one, "To your offspring", which is Christ. Now I say this: A covenant confirmed beforehand by God in Christ, the law, which came four hundred thirty years after, does not annul, so as to make the promise of no effect. For if the inheritance is of the law, it is no more of promise; but God has granted it to Abraham by promise.

Then why is there the law? It was added because of transgressions, until the offspring should come to whom the promise has been made. It was ordained through angels by the hand of a mediator. Now a mediator is not between one, but God is one. Is the law then against the promises of God? Certainly not! For if there had been a law given which could make alive, most certainly righteousness would have been of the law. But the Scripture imprisoned all things under sin, that the promise by faith in Jesus Christ might be given to those who believe.

But before faith came, we were kept in custody under the law, confined for the faith which should afterwards be revealed. So that the law has become our tutor to bring us to Christ, that we might be justified by faith. But now that faith has come, we are no longer under a tutor. For you are all children of God, through faith in Christ Jesus. For as many of you as were baptized into Christ have put on Christ. There is neither Jew nor Greek, there is neither slave nor free man, there is neither male nor female; for you are all one in Christ Jesus. If you are Christ's, then you are Abraham's offspring and heirs according to promise.

But I say that so long as the heir is a child, he is no different from a bondservant, though he is lord of all, but is under guardians and stewards until the day appointed by the father. So we also, when we were children, were held in bondage under the elemental principles of the world. But when the fullness of the time came, God sent out his Son, born to a woman, born under the law, that he might redeem those who were under the law, that we might receive the adoption as children. And because you are children, God sent out the Spirit of his Son into your hearts, crying, "Abba, Father!" So you are no longer a bondservant, but a son; and if a son, then an heir of God through Christ.

However at that time, not knowing God, you were in bondage to those who by nature are not gods. But now that you have come to know God, or rather to be known by God, why do you turn back again to the weak and miserable elemental principles, to which you desire to be in bondage all over again? You observe days, months, seasons, and years. I am afraid for you, that I might have wasted my labor for you.

I beg you, brothers, become as I am, for I also have become as you are. You did me no wrong, but you know that because of weakness in the flesh I preached the Good News to you the first time. That which was a temptation to you in my flesh, you didn't despise nor reject; but you received me as an angel of God, even as Christ Jesus.

What was the blessing you enjoyed? For I testify to you that, if possible, you would have plucked out your eyes and given them to me. So then, have I become your enemy by telling you the truth? They zealously seek you in no good way. No, they desire to alienate you, that you may seek them. But it is always good to be zealous in a good cause, and not only when I am present with you.

My little children, of whom I am again in travail until Christ is formed in you— but I could wish to be present with you now, and to change my tone, for I am perplexed about you.

Tell me, you that desire to be under the law, don't you listen to the law? For it is written that Abraham had two sons, one by the servant, and one by the free woman. However, the son by the servant was born according to the flesh, but the son by the free woman was born through promise. These things contain an allegory, for these are two covenants. One is from Mount Sinai, bearing children to bondage, which is Hagar. For this Hagar is Mount Sinai in Arabia, and answers to the Jerusalem that exists now, for she is in bondage with her children. But the Jerusalem that is above is free, which is the mother of us all. For it is written,

"Rejoice, you barren who don't bear.

>Break out and shout, you who don't travail.
>
>For the desolate have more children than her who has a husband."

Now we, brothers, as Isaac was, are children of promise. But as then, he who was born according to the flesh persecuted him who was born according to the Spirit, so also it is now. However what does the Scripture say? "Throw out the servant and her son, for the son of the servant will not inherit with the son of the free woman." So then, brothers, we are not children of a servant, but of the free woman.

Stand firm therefore in the liberty by which Christ has made us free, and don't be entangled again with a yoke of bondage.

Behold, I, Paul, tell you that if you receive circumcision, Christ will profit you nothing. Yes, I testify again to every man who receives circumcision that he is a debtor to do the whole law. You are alienated from Christ, you who desire to be justified by the law. You have fallen away from grace. For we, through the Spirit, by faith wait for the hope of righteousness. For in Christ Jesus neither circumcision amounts to anything, nor uncircumcision, but faith working through love. You were running well! Who interfered with you that you should not obey the truth? This persuasion is not from him who calls you. A little yeast grows through the whole lump. I have confidence toward you in the Lord that you will think no other way. But he who troubles you will bear his judgment, whoever he is.

But I, brothers, if I still preach circumcision, why am I still persecuted? Then the stumbling block of the cross has been removed. I wish that those who disturb you would cut themselves off.

For you, brothers, were called for freedom. Only don't use your freedom for gain to the flesh, but through love be servants to one another. For the whole law is fulfilled in one word, in this: "You shall love your neighbor as yourself." But if you bite and devour one another, be careful that you don't consume one another.

But I say, walk by the Spirit, and you won't fulfill the lust of the flesh. For the flesh lusts against the Spirit, and the Spirit against the flesh; and these are contrary to one another, that you may not do the things that you desire. But if you are led by the Spirit, you are not under the law. Now the deeds of the flesh are obvious, which are: adultery, sexual immorality, uncleanness, lustfulness, idolatry, sorcery, hatred, strife, jealousies, outbursts of anger, rivalries, divisions, heresies, envy, murders, drunkenness, orgies, and things like these; of which I forewarn you, even as I also forewarned you, that those who practice such things will not inherit God's Kingdom. But the fruit of the Spirit is love, joy, peace, patience, kindness, goodness, faith, gentleness, and self-control. Against such things there is no law. Those who belong to Christ have crucified the flesh with its passions and lusts.

If we live by the Spirit, let's also walk by the Spirit. Let's not become conceited, provoking one another, and envying one another.

Brothers, even if a man is caught in some fault, you who are spiritual must restore such a one in a spirit of gentleness; looking to yourself so that you also aren't tempted. Bear one another's burdens, and so fulfill the law of Christ. For if a man thinks himself to be something when he is nothing, he deceives himself. But let each man examine his own work, and then he will have reason to boast in himself, and not in someone else. For each man will bear his own burden. But let him who is taught in the word share all good things with him who teaches. Don't be deceived. God is not mocked, for whatever a man sows, that he will also reap. For he who sows to his own flesh will from the flesh reap corruption. But he who sows to the Spirit will from the Spirit reap eternal life. Let's not be weary in doing good, for we will reap in due season, if we don't give up. So then, as we have opportunity, let's do what is good toward all men, and especially toward those who are of the household of the faith.

See with what large letters I write to you with my own hand. As many as desire to make a good impression in the flesh compel you to be circumcised; just so they may not be persecuted for the cross of Christ. For even they who receive circumcision don't keep the law themselves, but they desire to have you circumcised, that they may boast in your flesh. But far be it from me to boast, except in the cross of our Lord Jesus Christ, through which the world has been crucified to me, and I to the world. For in Christ Jesus neither is circumcision anything, nor uncircumcision, but a new creation. As many as walk by this rule, peace and mercy be on them, and on God's Israel. From now on, let no one cause me any trouble, for I bear the marks of the Lord Jesus branded on my body.

The grace of our Lord Jesus Christ be with your spirit, brothers. Amen.

Revealed Journal

Journal pages are where you will summarize, observe, and outline your passage for study. You will collect your research for L I F E and unpack *What is Revealed* in the passage. Then you are ready to L I V E in light of God's revelation.

Instructions

I: Revealed Passage - At the top of the page, write the book, chapter, and verses of your bracketed section. Each main idea section you just identified is a Revealed Passage. Most Revealed Passage sections will be between 8-20 verses in length.

II: Verse Summaries - Summarize each verse in your Revealed Passage by re-writing the passage into shorter phrases. You are recording key words and information. Keep it simple, aiming to have less statements than verses. This step is essential to observing and outlining the passage.

III: Observations and Questions - Jot down observations and questions as you go. Use the list below to guide you. Fill it up, color code it, scribble away!

- Characters: descriptions, details, behaviors, attitudes
- Actions and responses
- Words that are repeated or emphasized
- Comparisons and contrasts
- Cause and effect: *therefore, since,* and *if-then* type statements
- Figures of speech: simile, metaphor, idiom, hyperbole, etc.
- Questions and answer
- Dialogue: who is talking to whom
- Emotion or tone
- Confusing words, phrases, or actions

IV: Revealed Outline. Condense your verse summaries into 3-5 main points to create an outline of the Revealed Passage.

V: One Sentence: Use your Revealed Outline to craft one sentence that encapsulates your Revealed Passage. This one sentence is a summary of the whole passage and should be recognizable to the original author and audience. Be specific when you can by using the author's name, main characters, or identifying events.

28

...continued

VI: Revealing L I F E: It's time to work toward a solid interpretation guided by the hermeneutical principals of L I F E.

L - Let the original author speak to the original audience. These ancient texts were not written TO us. They were written FOR us but must always be read and understood from their original historical and cultural context- author and audience. What does the text reveal of the author? What does the text reveal about the audience? What is taking place in history? What do we know from other sources and archeology about that time, place, and people? What were their values, worldviews, and cultural distinctions? All these questions help us *let the original author speak to the original audience.*

I - Investigate words and sentences within paragraphs. The authors of all 66 books of the Bible used regular communication methods for their day. To interpret ordinary written communication, we want to understand the smallest literary unit that holds meaning in that text. We know that the words we use change meaning, tone, and intention based on their literary context, words within sentences, sentences within paragraphs, and paragraphs within essays. Our outline aids us greatly here as we *investigate words and sentences within their communicated context.*

F - Fill in gaps from outside sources. The world of the ancient Near East is very different from today. From customs and cultural practices to the common imagery used in the biblical texts, we need to fill in the gaps between then and now. Using outside resources, we can uncover and overcome these differences. The information available to us today provides a wealth of scholars, experts, and research at our fingertips. Refer to the resources listed in the back to *fill in the gaps from outside sources.*

E- Explore the bigger picture and similar passages. There are over 40 biblical authors, writing over 1500 years, so consider your passage with the whole counsel of God's revelation in view. This last guiding principal asks us to compare parallel passages and the rest of the biblical context. What has gone before and what comes after this text? Where else is this theme or message presented? Are there other passages that affirm or explain this passage? Asking these questions helps us to *explore the bigger picture.*

...continued

VII: What is Revealed? Now that you have followed L I F E through your passage, ask yourself what theological principal or truth is revealed in this passage. What truth reaches out of their day into ours? The Bible speaks to both a specific place and time in history AND holds eternal relevance and truth for today. This lasting truth or principal will be what you aim to L I V E through application. What is revealed about God? Humanity? Salvation? Creation? Etc. Write your Revealed statement in this section and flip to the back *What was Revealed* pages to keep a running collection of truths from your study.

VIII: L I V E Revealed: We have done a lot of work to get to this point. We sought to be faithful to original intent of the passage and spent time in prayer and research to understand its implications for us today. The real work starts now. All of our efforts amount to nothing if we go on living unchanged lives. Every truth of Scripture confronts us and leaves us with a choice. The steps of L I V E are intentional ways we can respond to *What is Revealed*.

- **L- <u>Let the lesson linger</u>.** Keep the conversation going with God even after you've closed your journal. Look for connections in everyday life and chew on what is revealed. This act of going over and working every angle is what biblical meditation is all about. Fill your mind, feast of God's words, and let it soak into your heart. What am I going to do with this truth? Transformation takes time. This principal encourages us to look for connections, opportunities, and examples in our own lives and to put what is revealed on repeat. Don't rush on if it hasn't hit home. *Let the lesson linger.*

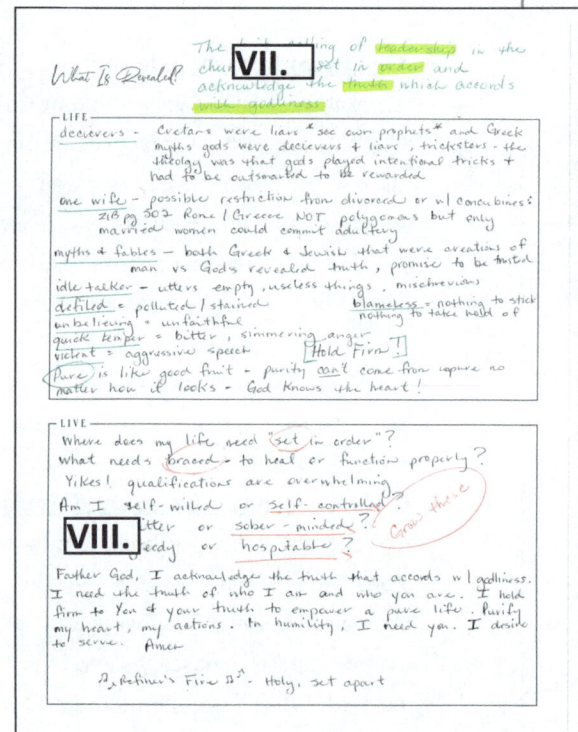

- **I- <u>Invite in community</u>.** Whatever this might look like for you, don't neglect growing with other believers. Share with friends and family the passage you are studying and what you see being revealed. Ask others to share their thoughts and perspectives. Compare your journal with other teachings on that passage. Who could you share this lesson with? Do you need accountability or help? God has given us other believers to encourage, equip, challenge, and sharpen us. Where can you *invite in community*?

...continued

V- <u>Voice the truth</u>. Say it out-loud. Pray and personalize the message. Speaking and hearing activate the brain differently than reading and sight alone. Be creative! Memorize a key verse from your passage, write your Revealed statement on a post-it note and plaster it around your house, recite these truths while you sit in traffic, write a poem, or sing a song. Ask God in prayer to help empower you and *voice the truth*.

E- <u>Enter into worship</u>. This is the only logical conclusion of our time with God in His word. Everything we have done up to this point has been preparing our minds and hearts to worship. Worship is active, our response to God's revelation. What is your response? How has your heart been led to praise, thanksgiving, obedience, song, or service? Where can you give generously today? What needs to be surrendered? Go on – *Enter into worship*!

Revealed Passage:

Observations & Questions

Verse Summaries

Revealed Passage Outline

One Sentence

What Is Revealed?

LIFE

LIVE

Revealed Passage:

Observations & Questions

Verse Summaries

Revealed Passage Outline

One Sentence

What Is Revealed?

LIFE

LIVE

Revealed Passage:

Observations & Questions

Verse Summaries

Revealed Passage Outline

One Sentence

What Is Revealed?

LIFE

LIVE

Revealed Passage:

Observations & Questions

Verse Summaries

Revealed Passage Outline

One Sentence

What Is Revealed?

LIFE

LIVE

Revealed Passage:

Observations & Questions

Verse Summaries

Revealed Passage Outline

One Sentence

What Is Revealed?

LIFE

LIVE

Revealed Passage:

Observations & Questions

Verse Summaries

Revealed Passage Outline

One Sentence

What Is Revealed?

LIFE

LIVE

Revealed Passage:

Observations & Questions

Verse Summaries

Revealed Passage Outline

One Sentence

What Is Revealed?

LIFE

LIVE

Revealed Passage:

Observations & Questions

Verse Summaries

Revealed Passage Outline

One Sentence

What Is Revealed?

LIFE

LIVE

Revealed Passage:

Observations & Questions

Verse Summaries

Revealed Passage Outline

One Sentence

What Is Revealed?

LIFE

LIVE

Revealed Passage:

Observations & Questions

Verse Summaries

Revealed Passage Outline

One Sentence

What Is Revealed?

LIFE

LIVE

Revealed Passage:

Observations & Questions

Verse Summaries

Revealed Passage Outline

One Sentence

What Is Revealed?

LIFE

LIVE

Revealed Passage:

Observations & Questions

Verse Summaries

Revealed Passage Outline

One Sentence

What Is Revealed?

LIFE

LIVE

Revealed Passage:

Observations & Questions

Verse Summaries

Revealed Passage Outline

One Sentence

What Is Revealed?

LIFE

LIVE

Revealed Passage:

Observations & Questions

Verse Summaries

Revealed Passage Outline

One Sentence

What Is Revealed?

LIFE

LIVE

Ephesians

Prepare: Ephesians

Gather Context

The first step to studying any passage of Scripture is gathering context. For each book you will study, understanding the larger context is essential to sound interpretation. The best way to gather context is by **reading the whole book**! You can read or listen to the audio book in your favorite version. The purpose is to see the broader story from beginning to end before digging beneath the surface. Refer to a few outside resources to answer the inital context questions below in the boxes on the next page.

- Who is the author(s) and audience?
- What do you know about them?
- Where is the author and audience?
- What are the key features of their location?
- When was this book written?
- When did the events in the book take place?

- When did the events take place in terms of redemptive history or the bigger narrative of Scripture? Exile, Exodus, church age, etc
- What is the main genre of this book? Narrative, law, poetry, etc.
- What are the key features of this book?

Pray for Wisdom

You won't notice prayer as a separate step listed in this method. Prayer isn't a piece of the process, it permeates the process. Prayer is a two-way conversation with God: honest sharing and reflective listening. Prayer acts like the canvas on which the painting is created. God doesn't begin to listen at 'Dear Heavenly Father' and shut off at 'Amen'. Acknowledge His presence always. Ask for wisdom and understanding. From start to finish, we are in conversation with the One revealing Himself to us.

Who

Where

When

Genre

Divide

Instructions

For each book in this journal, you will find a copy of the World English Bible (WEB) translation with all chapter and verse marks removed. Why? Because **you** will do the work of dividing the passage into sections for yourself! The goal is to break each book into smaller sections to study in your Revealed Journal.

The chapter and verse markings in your Bible are not inspired and are placed there to make passages easier to read and reference. Sub-headings are the translator's attempt at dividing up longer passages into smaller stories or main ideas, but these are not original to the biblical texts. Reading Scripture with these markings removed allows us to find the main ideas for ourselves. It gives us as modern readers a good starting point for reading the text as the original audience would have received it.

So turn to the book you are studying, grab a pencil, and start placing brackets in the margin where you think a main idea starts and stops. Look for clues in the text that indicate a change in subject, location, tone, etc. **Group together verses and paragraphs that cover one big idea, singular event, or key theological concept.** Once you have a few pages marked, grab the Bible translation you plan to use for your study and compare your bracketed sections. Write the corresponding chapter and verse numbers along your bracketed margin. These sections will be the Revealed Passages you work through in your journal. Reference the sample in the back if needed. With larger books, its best to divide a few pages and then start journaling. Ephesians is a smaller book, so try and divide the whole book before beginning your journaling.

The WEB copy in your journal also gives you the opportunity to mark up your observations on your subsequent readings. Use different colored pens to circle key words, underline main ideas, or highlight questions. Some people are more hesitant to mark up their actual Bible, but feel free to mark up this copy however you like!

Ephesians

Paul, an apostle of Christ Jesus through the will of God, to the saints who are at Ephesus, and the faithful in Christ Jesus: Grace to you and peace from God our Father and the Lord Jesus Christ.

Blessed be the God and Father of our Lord Jesus Christ, who has blessed us with every spiritual blessing in the heavenly places in Christ, even as he chose us in him before the foundation of the world, that we would be holy and without defect before him in love, having predestined us for adoption as children through Jesus Christ to himself, according to the good pleasure of his desire, to the praise of the glory of his grace, by which he freely gave us favor in the Beloved, in whom we have our redemption through his blood, the forgiveness of our trespasses, according to the riches of his grace, which he made to abound toward us in all wisdom and prudence, making known to us the mystery of his will, according to his good pleasure which he purposed in him to an administration of the fullness of the times, to sum up all things in Christ, the things in the heavens and the things on the earth, in him. We were also assigned an inheritance in him, having been foreordained according to the purpose of him who does all things after the counsel of his will, to the end that we should be to the praise of his glory, we who had before hoped in Christ. In him you also, having heard the word of the truth, the Good News of your salvation—in whom, having also believed, you were sealed with the promised Holy Spirit, who is a pledge of our inheritance, to the redemption of God's own possession, to the praise of his glory.

For this cause I also, having heard of the faith in the Lord Jesus which is among you, and the love which you have toward all the saints, don't cease to give thanks for you, making mention of you in my prayers, that the God of our Lord Jesus Christ, the Father of glory, may give to you a spirit of wisdom and revelation in the knowledge of him, having the eyes of your hearts enlightened, that you may know what is the hope of his calling, and what are the riches of the glory of his inheritance in the saints, and what is the exceeding greatness of his power toward us who believe, according to that working of the strength of his might which he worked in Christ, when he raised him from the dead and made him to sit at his right hand in the heavenly places, far above all rule, authority, power, dominion, and every name that is named, not only in this age, but also in that which is to come. He put all things in subjection under his feet, and gave him to be head over all things for the assembly, which is his body, the fullness of him who fills all in all.

You were made alive when you were dead in transgressions and sins, in which you once walked according to the course of this world, according to the prince of the power of the air, the spirit who now works in the children of disobedience. We also all once lived among them in the lusts of our flesh, doing the desires of the flesh and of the mind, and were by nature children of wrath, even as the rest. But God, being rich in mercy, for his great love with which he loved us, even when we were dead through our trespasses, made us alive together with Christ—by grace you have been saved— and raised us up with him, and made us to sit with him in the heavenly places in Christ Jesus, that in the ages to come he might show the exceeding riches of his grace in kindness toward us in Christ Jesus; for by grace you have been saved through faith, and that not of yourselves; it is the gift of God, not of works, that no one would boast. For we are his workmanship, created in Christ Jesus for good works, which God prepared before that we would walk in them.

Therefore remember that once you, the Gentiles in the flesh, who are called "uncircumcision" by that which is called "circumcision" (in the flesh, made by hands), that you were at that time separate from Christ, alienated from the commonwealth of Israel, and strangers from the covenants of the promise, having no hope and without God in the world. But now in Christ Jesus you who once were far off are made near in the blood of Christ. For he is our peace, who made both one, and broke down the middle wall of separation, having abolished in his flesh the hostility, the law of commandments contained in ordinances, that he might create in himself one new man of the two, making peace, and might reconcile them both in one body to God through the cross, having killed the hostility through it. He came and preached peace to you who were far off and to those who were near. For through him we both have our access in one Spirit to the Father. So then you are no longer strangers and foreigners, but you are fellow citizens with the saints and of the household of God, being built on the foundation of the apostles and prophets, Christ Jesus himself being the chief cornerstone; in whom the whole building, fitted together, grows into a holy temple in the Lord; in whom you also are built together for a habitation of God in the Spirit. For this cause I, Paul, am the prisoner of Christ Jesus on behalf of you Gentiles, if it is so that you have heard of the administration of that grace of God which was given me toward you, how that by revelation the mystery was made known to me, as I wrote before in few words, by which, when you read, you can perceive my understanding in the mystery of Christ, which in other generations was not made known to the children of men, as it has now been revealed to his holy apostles and prophets in the Spirit, that the Gentiles are fellow heirs and fellow members of the body, and fellow partakers of his promise in Christ Jesus through the Good News, of which I was made a servant according to the gift of that grace of God which was given me according to the working of his power. To me, the very least of all saints, was this grace given, to preach to the Gentiles the unsearchable riches of Christ, and to make all men see what is the administration of the mystery which for ages has been hidden in God, who created all things through Jesus Christ, to the intent that now through the assembly the manifold wisdom of God might be made known to the principalities and the powers in the heavenly places, according to the eternal purpose which he accomplished in Christ Jesus our Lord. In him we have boldness and access in confidence through our faith in him. Therefore I ask that you may not lose heart at my troubles for you, which are your glory.

For this cause, I bow my knees to the Father of our Lord Jesus Christ, from whom every family in heaven and on earth is named, that he would grant you, according to the riches of his glory, that you may be strengthened with power through his Spirit in the inner person, that Christ may dwell in your hearts through faith, to the end that you, being rooted and grounded in love, may be strengthened to comprehend with all the saints what is the width and length and height and depth, and to know Christ's love which surpasses knowledge, that you may be filled with all the fullness of God.

Now to him who is able to do exceedingly abundantly above all that we ask or think, according to the power that works in us, to him be the glory in the assembly and in Christ Jesus to all generations forever and ever. Amen.

I therefore, the prisoner in the Lord, beg you to walk worthily of the calling with which you were called, with all lowliness and humility, with patience, bearing with one another in love, being eager to keep the unity of the Spirit in the bond of peace. There is one body and one Spirit, even as you also were called in one hope of your calling, one Lord, one faith, one baptism, one God and Father of all, who is over all and through all, and in us all. But to each one of us, the grace was given according to the measure of the gift of Christ. Therefore he says,

"When he ascended on high,

   he led captivity captive,

   and gave gifts to people."

Now this, "He ascended", what is it but that he also first descended into the lower parts of the earth? He who descended is the one who also ascended far above all the heavens, that he might fill all things.

He gave some to be apostles; and some, prophets; and some, evangelists; and some, shepherds[a] and teachers; for the perfecting of the saints, to the work of serving, to the building up of the body of Christ, until we all attain to the unity of the faith and of the knowledge of the Son of God, to a full grown man, to the measure of the stature of the fullness of Christ, that we may no longer be children, tossed back and forth and carried about with every wind of doctrine, by the trickery of men, in craftiness, after the wiles of error; but speaking truth in love, we may grow up in all things into him who is the head, Christ, from whom all the body, being fitted and knit together through that which every joint supplies, according to the working in measure of each individual part, makes the body increase to the building up of itself in love.

This I say therefore, and testify in the Lord, that you no longer walk as the rest of the Gentiles also walk, in the futility of their mind, being darkened in their understanding, alienated from the life of God because of the ignorance that is in them, because of the hardening of their hearts. They, having become callous, gave themselves up to lust, to work all uncleanness with greediness. But you didn't learn Christ that way, if indeed you heard him, and were taught in him, even as truth is in Jesus: that you put away, as concerning your former way of life, the old man that grows corrupt after the lusts of deceit, and that you be renewed in the spirit of your mind, and put on the new man, who in the likeness of God has been created in righteousness and holiness of truth.

Therefore putting away falsehood, speak truth each one with his neighbor. For we are members of one another. "Be angry, and don't sin." Don't let the sun go down on your wrath, and don't give place to the devil. Let him who stole steal no more; but rather let him labor, producing with his hands something that is good, that he may have something to give to him who has need. Let no corrupt speech proceed out of your mouth, but only what is good for building others up as the need may be, that it may give grace to those who hear. Don't grieve the Holy Spirit of God, in whom you were sealed for the day of redemption. Let all bitterness, wrath, anger, outcry, and slander be put away from you, with all malice. And be kind to one another, tender hearted, forgiving each other, just as God also in Christ forgave you.

Be therefore imitators of God, as beloved children. Walk in love, even as Christ also loved us and gave himself up for us, an offering and a sacrifice to God for a sweet-smelling fragrance.

But sexual immorality, and all uncleanness or covetousness, let it not even be mentioned among you, as becomes saints; nor filthiness, nor foolish talking, nor jesting, which are not appropriate, but rather giving of thanks.

Know this for sure, that no sexually immoral person, nor unclean person, nor covetous man, who is an idolater, has any inheritance in the Kingdom of Christ and God.

Let no one deceive you with empty words. For because of these things, the wrath of God comes on the children of disobedience. Therefore don't be partakers with them. For you were once darkness, but are now light in the Lord. Walk as children of light, for the fruit of the Spirit is in all goodness and righteousness and truth, proving what is well pleasing to the Lord.

Have no fellowship with the unfruitful deeds of darkness, but rather even reprove them. For it is a shame even to speak of the things which are done by them in secret. But all things, when they are reproved, are revealed by the light, for everything that reveals is light. Therefore he says, "Awake, you who sleep, and arise from the dead, and Christ will shine on you."

Therefore watch carefully how you walk, not as unwise, but as wise, redeeming the time, because the days are evil. Therefore don't be foolish, but understand what the will of the Lord is. Don't be drunken with wine, in which is dissipation, but be filled with the Spirit, speaking to one another in psalms, hymns, and spiritual songs; singing and making melody in your heart to the Lord; giving thanks always concerning all things in the name of our Lord Jesus Christ, to God, even the Father; subjecting yourselves to one another in the fear of Christ.

Wives, be subject to your own husbands, as to the Lord. For the husband is the head of the wife, as Christ also is the head of the assembly, being himself the savior of the body. But as the assembly is subject to Christ, so let the wives also be to their own husbands in everything.

Husbands, love your wives, even as Christ also loved the assembly, and gave himself up for it; that he might sanctify it, having cleansed it by the washing of water with the word, that he might present the assembly to himself gloriously, not having spot or wrinkle or any such thing; but that it should be holy and without defect. Even so husbands also ought to love their own wives as their own bodies. He who loves his own wife loves himself. For no man ever hated his own flesh; but nourishes and cherishes it, even as the Lord also does the assembly; because we are members of his body, of his flesh and bones. "For this cause a man will leave his father and mother, and will be joined to his wife. Then the two will become one flesh." This mystery is great, but I speak concerning Christ and of the assembly. Nevertheless each of you must also love his own wife even as himself; and let the wife see that she respects her husband.

Children, obey your parents in the Lord, for this is right. "Honor your father and mother," which is the first commandment with a promise: "that it may be well with you, and you may live long on the earth."

You fathers, don't provoke your children to wrath, but nurture them in the discipline and instruction of the Lord.

Servants, be obedient to those who according to the flesh are your masters, with fear and trembling, in singleness of your heart, as to Christ, not in the way of service only when eyes are on you, as men pleasers, but as servants of Christ, doing the will of God from the heart, with good will doing service as to the Lord, and not to men, knowing that whatever good thing each one does, he will receive the same good again from the Lord, whether he is bound or free.

You masters, do the same things to them, and give up threatening, knowing that he who is both their Master and yours is in heaven, and there is no partiality with him.

Finally, be strong in the Lord, and in the strength of his might. Put on the whole armor of God, that you may be able to stand against the wiles of the devil. For our wrestling is not against flesh and blood, but against the principalities, against the powers, against the world's rulers of the darkness of this age, and against the spiritual forces of wickedness in the heavenly places. Therefore put on the whole armor of God, that you may be able to withstand in the evil day, and having done all, to stand. Stand therefore, having the utility belt of truth buckled around your waist, and having put on the breastplate of righteousness, and having fitted your feet with the preparation of the Good News of peace, above all, taking up the shield of faith, with which you will be able to quench all the fiery darts of the evil one. And take the helmet of salvation, and the sword of the Spirit, which is the word[a] of God; with all prayer and requests, praying at all times in the Spirit, and being watchful to this end in all perseverance and requests for all the saints: on my behalf, that utterance may be given to me in opening my mouth, to make known with boldness the mystery of the Good News, for which I am an ambassador in chains; that in it I may speak boldly, as I ought to speak.

But that you also may know my affairs, how I am doing, Tychicus, the beloved brother and faithful servant in the Lord, will make known to you all things. I have sent him to you for this very purpose, that you may know our state and that he may comfort your hearts.

Peace be to the brothers, and love with faith, from God the Father and the Lord Jesus Christ.

Grace be with all those who love our Lord Jesus Christ with incorruptible love. Amen.

Revealed Journal

Journal pages are where you will summarize, observe, and outline your passage for study. You will collect your research for L I F E and unpack *What is Revealed* in the passage. Then you are ready to L I V E in light of God's revelation.

Instructions

I: Revealed Passage - At the top of the page, write the book, chapter, and verses of your bracketed section. Each main idea section you just identified is a Revealed Passage. Most Revealed Passage sections will be between 8-20 verses in length.

II: Verse Summaries - Summarize each verse in your Revealed Passage by re-writing the passage into shorter phrases. You are recording key words and information. Keep it simple, aiming to have less statements than verses. This step is essential to observing and outlining the passage.

III: Observations and Questions - Jot down observations and questions as you go. Use the list below to guide you. Fill it up, color code it, scribble away!

- Characters: descriptions, details, behaviors, attitudes
- Actions and responses
- Words that are repeated or emphasized
- Comparisons and contrasts
- Cause and effect: *therefore, since,* and *if-then* type statements
- Figures of speech: simile, metaphor, idiom, hyperbole, etc.
- Questions and answer
- Dialogue: who is talking to whom
- Emotion or tone
- Confusing words, phrases, or actions

IV: Revealed Outline. Condense your verse summaries into 3-5 main points to create an outline of the Revealed Passage.

V: One Sentence: Use your Revealed Outline to craft one sentence that encapsulates your Revealed Passage. This one sentence is a summary of the whole passage and should be recognizable to the original author and audience. Be specific when you can by using the author's name, main characters, or identifying events.

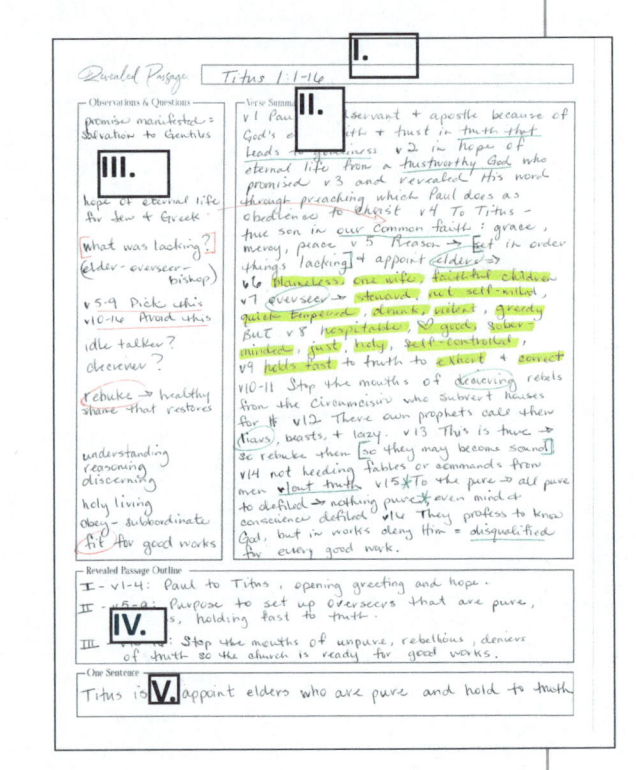

74

...continued

VI: Revealing L I F E: It's time to work toward a solid interpretation guided by the hermeneutical principals of L I F E.

L - Let the original author speak to the original audience. These ancient texts were not written TO us. They were written FOR us but must always be read and understood from their original historical and cultural context- author and audience. What does the text reveal of the author? What does the text reveal about the audience? What is taking place in history? What do we know from other sources and archeology about that time, place, and people? What were their values, worldviews, and cultural distinctions? All these questions help us *let the original author speak to the original audience.*

I - Investigate words and sentences within paragraphs. The authors of all 66 books of the Bible used regular communication methods for their day. To interpret ordinary written communication, we want to understand the smallest literary unit that holds meaning in that text. We know that the words we use change meaning, tone, and intention based on their literary context, words within sentences, sentences within paragraphs, and paragraphs within essays. Our outline aids us greatly here as we *investigate words and sentences within their communicated context.*

F - Fill in gaps from outside sources. The world of the ancient Near East is very different from today. From customs and cultural practices to the common imagery used in the biblical texts, we need to fill in the gaps between then and now. Using outside resources, we can uncover and overcome these differences. The information available to us today provides a wealth of scholars, experts, and research at our fingertips. Refer to the resources listed in the back to *fill in the gaps from outside sources.*

E- Explore the bigger picture and similar passages. There are over 40 biblical authors, writing over 1500 years, so consider your passage with the whole counsel of God's revelation in view. This last guiding principal asks us to compare parallel passages and the rest of the biblical context. What has gone before and what comes after this text? Where else is this theme or message presented? Are there other passages that affirm or explain this passage? Asking these questions helps us to *explore the bigger picture.*

75

...continued

VII: What is Revealed? Now that you have followed L I F E through your passage, ask yourself what theological principal or truth is revealed in this passage. What truth reaches out of their day into ours? The Bible speaks to both a specific place and time in history AND holds eternal relevance and truth for today. This lasting truth or principal will be what you aim to L I V E through application. What is revealed about God? Humanity? Salvation? Creation? Etc. Write your Revealed statement in this section and flip to the back *What was Revealed* pages to keep a running collection of truths from your study.

VIII: L I V E Revealed: We have done a lot of work to get to this point. We sought to be faithful to original intent of the passage and spent time in prayer and research to understand its implications for us today. The real work starts now. All of our efforts amount to nothing if we go on living unchanged lives. Every truth of Scripture confronts us and leaves us with a choice. The steps of L I V E are intentional ways we can respond to *What is Revealed*.

- **L- <u>Let the lesson linger.</u>** Keep the conversation going with God even after you've closed your journal. Look for connections in everyday life and chew on what is revealed. This act of going over and working every angle is what biblical meditation is all about. Fill your mind, feast of God's words, and let it soak into your heart. What am I going to do with this truth? Transformation takes time. This principal encourages us to look for connections, opportunities, and examples in our own lives and to put what is revealed on repeat. Don't rush on if it hasn't hit home. *Let the lesson linger.*

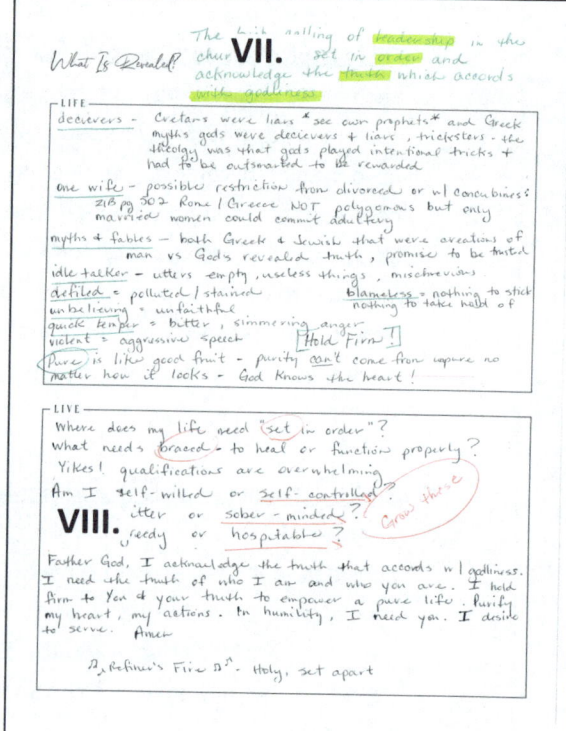

- **I- <u>Invite in community.</u>** Whatever this might look like for you, don't neglect growing with other believers. Share with friends and family the passage you are studying and what you see being revealed. Ask others to share their thoughts and perspectives. Compare your journal with other teachings on that passage. Who could you share this lesson with? Do you need accountability or help? God has given us other believers to encourage, equip, challenge, and sharpen us. Where can you *invite in community*?

76

...continued

V- <u>Voice the truth</u>. Say it out-loud. Pray and personalize the message. Speaking and hearing activate the brain differently than reading and sight alone. Be creative! Memorize a key verse from your passage, write your Revealed statement on a post-it note and plaster it around your house, recite these truths while you sit in traffic, write a poem, or sing a song. Ask God in prayer to help empower you and *voice the truth*.

E- <u>Enter into worship</u>. This is the only logical conclusion of our time with God in His word. Everything we have done up to this point has been preparing our minds and hearts to worship. Worship is active, our response to God's revelation. What is your response? How has your heart been led to praise, thanksgiving, obedience, song, or service? Where can you give generously today? What needs to be surrendered? Go on – *Enter into worship*!

Revealed Passage:

Observations & Questions

Verse Summaries

Revealed Passage Outline

One Sentence

What Is Revealed?

LIFE

LIVE

Revealed Passage:

Observations & Questions

Verse Summaries

Revealed Passage Outline

One Sentence

What Is Revealed?

― LIFE ―

― LIVE ―

Revealed Passage:

Observations & Questions

Verse Summaries

Revealed Passage Outline

One Sentence

What Is Revealed?

― LIFE ―

― LIVE ―

Revealed Passage:

Observations & Questions

Verse Summaries

Revealed Passage Outline

One Sentence

What Is Revealed?

LIFE

LIVE

Revealed Passage:

Observations & Questions

Verse Summaries

Revealed Passage Outline

One Sentence

What Is Revealed?

LIFE

LIVE

Revealed Passage:

Observations & Questions

Verse Summaries

Revealed Passage Outline

One Sentence

What Is Revealed?

LIFE

LIVE

Revealed Passage:

Observations & Questions

Verse Summaries

Revealed Passage Outline

One Sentence

What Is Revealed?

LIFE

LIVE

Revealed Passage:

Observations & Questions

Verse Summaries

Revealed Passage Outline

One Sentence

What Is Revealed?

LIFE

LIVE

Revealed Passage:

Observations & Questions

Verse Summaries

Revealed Passage Outline

One Sentence

What Is Revealed?

LIFE

LIVE

Revealed Passage:

Observations & Questions

Verse Summaries

Revealed Passage Outline

One Sentence

What Is Revealed?

LIFE

LIVE

Revealed Passage:

Observations & Questions

Verse Summaries

Revealed Passage Outline

One Sentence

What Is Revealed?

LIFE

LIVE

Revealed Passage:

Observations & Questions

Verse Summaries

Revealed Passage Outline

One Sentence

What Is Revealed?

LIFE

LIVE

Revealed Passage:

Observations & Questions

Verse Summaries

Revealed Passage Outline

One Sentence

What Is Revealed?

LIFE

LIVE

Revealed Passage:

Observations & Questions

Verse Summaries

Revealed Passage Outline

One Sentence

What Is Revealed?

LIFE

LIVE

Revealed Truth: Galatians

Revealed Truth: Galatians

Revealed Truth: Ephesians

-
-
-
-
-
-
-
-
-
-
-
-
-
-
-
-
-
-

Revealed Truth: Ephesians

-
-
-
-
-
-
-
-
-
-
-
-
-
-
-
-
-
-
-

Resources

There are many resources available to us as we navigate L I F E. If you have an Internet capable device, you have a wealth of information at your fingertips. I recommend the following, but as you go, you'll figure out what options work best for you.

#1. Use multiple translations! There are a large variety of translations to choose from and I recommend different "types" of translations for different purposes. For your pre-reading or audio listening, try a dynamic equivalent translation or a trusted paraphrase. Paraphrases are often called free translations because while they are seeking to remain true to the original ideas of the text, there are liberties taken to put the text into the author's own words. Dynamic equivalent translations are called thought-for-thought translations and seek to find equivalent thoughts, ideas, and structures that make the text more readable for a modern audience. If the purpose is to get the big picture or read through a larger portion of Scripture, go with a dynamic equivalent translation. When the desire is a greater understanding of the meaning of a text, pull out a formal equivalent or literal translation. They seek to translate word for word, staying as close to the original language as possible. Formal equivalents are great for theological study. As modern readers, want to get the most out of our Bible study, so we need multiple translations. The WEB version included in your journal is a formal equivalent or word-for-word translation. Other popular translations are given below. If you don't see your favorite, find out what type of translation you are reading and add some diversity to your collection.

Parallel Bibles save time and money! A good parallel Bible will have each of the 3 types of translations listed in parallel or side-by-side for ease of reference. Most free online Bible sites also have parallel features so you can quickly read the passage in numerous versions.

Formal or Literal:	Dynamic:	Free:
ESV	NIV	TLB
NASB	NLT	NIrV
KJV	AMP	GNT
WEB	CSB	MSG

#2. Own a study Bible. — Look for a study Bible in a dynamic or formal equivalent translation. Study Bibles have historical notes, word definitions, maps, cross references, and more. A good study Bible will give you context and explain cultural differences. Pick your favorite, I like the NIV and ESV Study Bibles..

#3. Refer to a Bible dictionary, concordance, or lexicon. - These all help with word usage and are the most common resources used outside of the text. Many online options abound! Try blueletterbible.org and biblestudytools.com.

#4. Check imagery and cultural backgrounds. - I find background resources very helpful and unless you have a Bible software subscription like Logos, you will want to have a hard copy. *Dictionary of Biblical Imagery*, *Zondervan Illustrated Bible Backgrounds*, and *IVP Bible Backgrounds* are great options.

#5. Consult commentaries. - This can turn into a rabbit hole of endless online researching and reading. My recommendation is to stick to online options unless you are writing your own curriculum through a book of the Bible. Don't buy a commentary to study one passage. I prefer to read from various theological perspectives and from both modern and classic authors, but don't get lost in the weeds here. Ask your pastor or a trusted teacher what commentaries they like and go from there.

Online Gems!

blueletterbible.org – biblegateway.com – biblestudytools.com – gotquestions.org

freebiblecommentary.org - I have personally been heavily influenced by the approach and teaching of Dr. Utley. His written commentaries and video teachings are staples in my study!

Bible Project: for videos and amazing overview content- *bibleproject.com*

Genre Guide

Narrative

Narratives are purposeful stories that retell historical events to give meaning, direction, and remembrance for a current audience. The basic components of a narrative are the characters, plot - which includes the conflict or tension- and the resolution. In Hebrew narrative, God is always the protagonist and His enemies, both spiritual and earthly, are the antagonists. God's people and those who serve Him are the agonists, major characters who get involved in the struggle of the protagonist and antagonist. The narrator of any story is not a trivial role. They present the point of view and include details according to their intent. The story is moved along through scenes and the focus is usually on the characters and their dialogue to propel the plot. Ancient narrative is primarily for HEARERS, not readers. The author is retelling what happened, not necessarily moralizing what should have or ought to happen.

Law

In Scripture, "law" can refer to any one of the 600+ commands in Scripture. It can also be the collective group of commands or reference to the Pentateuch, the covenant laws and narrative context in which those laws were embedded. Laws are covenant agreements between two parties where BOTH have oligations to fulfill. There are moral, civil, and ritual/ceremonial laws given as the terms of the agreement between Isreal and Yahweh. The new covenant (NT) reaffirms and amends some of the old covenant (OT) but not all of it. The laws must be understood in their given context.

Gospels

The Gospel accounts give us 4 narrative perspectives on the life, teachings, and parables of Jesus. Think of them more as "memoirs of the apostles" than biographies of Jesus. There are many elements of "shared" work, but each author had an audience and purpose that impacted their choice of content and chronology. Comparing parallel passages is helpful as we remember the difference in purpose and perspective.

Parables are illustrative short stories or phrases that function to elicit a corrective response from the hearer. Most demonstrate the nature of the Kingdom of God and include cultural points of reference the audience would have understood to help make the point. Knowing who the intended audience was is important when studying parables.

Prophecy

Despite what you might think, the main function of the prophets was NOT fore-telling but forth-telling. They were to speak for God and were always calling His people back to covenant loyalty. Prophets were primarily convenant enforcement officers. When they were future-telling events, there was usually dual or multiple fulfillments: something current or soon-to-be fulfilled, something fulfilled in the Messiah, or something yet to be fulfilled. But the message was always the same- God always keeps His covenant. Yahweh is faithful, just, and true.

Wisdom

Wisdom literature is an ancient literary form concerned with right living. It includes proverbs, poems, dialogue, and narratives that teach godly living through generalizations of how the observable world works. Wisdom is what one seeks to gain by applying God's truth and learning from their experiences.

Poetry

Poetry utilizes figurative language, metaphor, simlie, and hyperbole. The most common feature of Hebrew poetry is parallelism, where an idea is first stated and then further deveoploed in "parallels". Poems are meant to invoke an emotional response by speaking to the head through the heart. They were used for worship, demonstrated how to relate honestly to God, and showed how to reflect and meditate on what God had done.

Letters

Letters or epistles are cooorespondence and teaching where we have half the conversation preserved. Each letter was occasional, meaning it was written to and for a specific occasion. Some were intended for public reading, circulation, and discourse, while others were rather private.

Apocalypse

Apocalyptic literary form isn't used today, but in ancient times it was occasional to persecution or threat and was concerned with judgement and salvation. Primarily hopeful, the imagery was fantastical and the language symbolic and cryptic. There is apocalyptic form througout the Bible, but the book of Revealtion is the most well-known. Revelation cites the OT over 250 times!

Divide Sample

1. Place brackets in the margin where you think a section starts and stops.

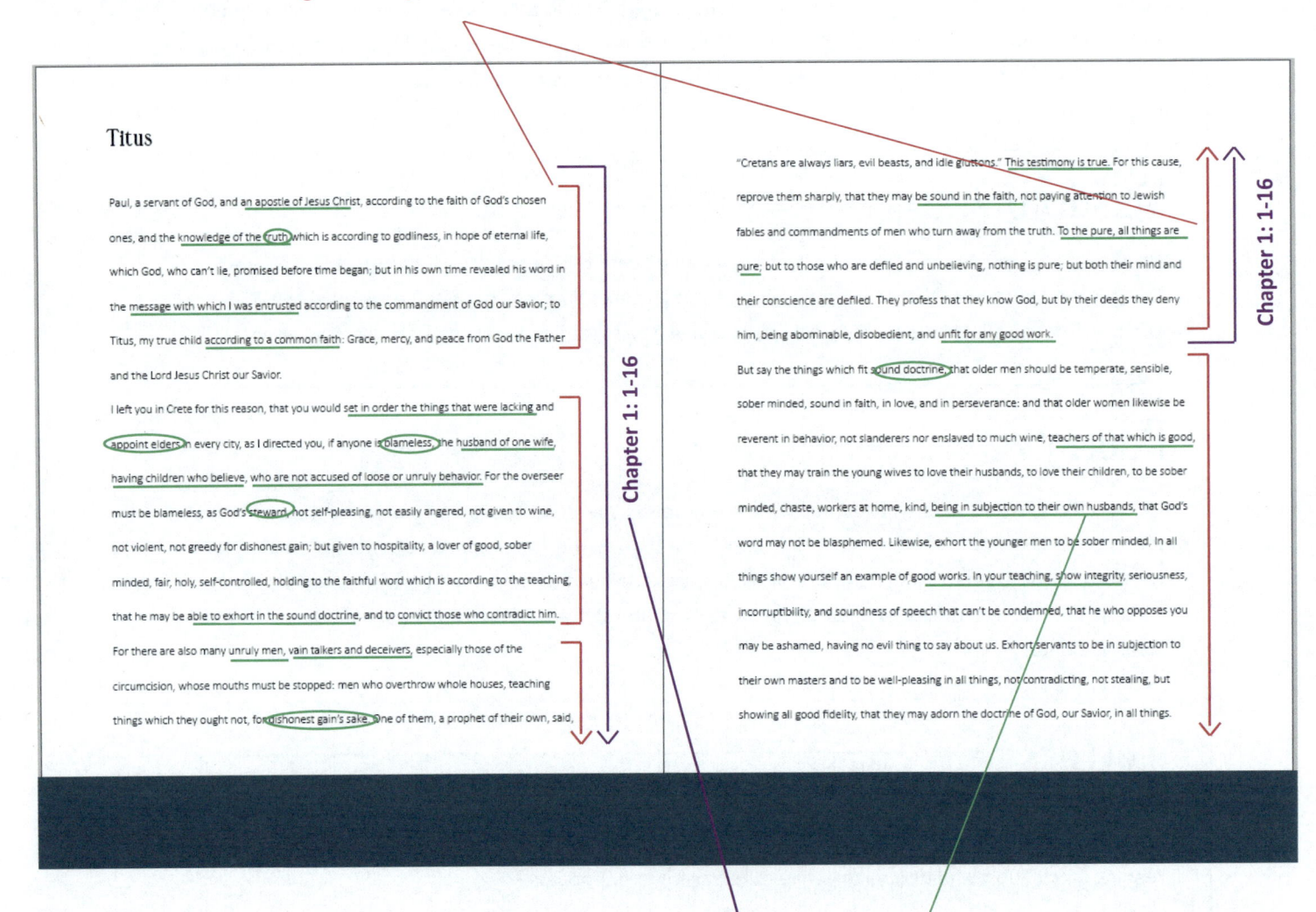

Titus

Paul, a servant of God, and an apostle of Jesus Christ, according to the faith of God's chosen ones, and the knowledge of the truth which is according to godliness, in hope of eternal life, which God, who can't lie, promised before time began; but in his own time revealed his word in the message with which I was entrusted according to the commandment of God our Savior; to Titus, my true child according to a common faith: Grace, mercy, and peace from God the Father and the Lord Jesus Christ our Savior.

I left you in Crete for this reason, that you would set in order the things that were lacking and appoint elders in every city, as I directed you, if anyone is blameless, the husband of one wife, having children who believe, who are not accused of loose or unruly behavior. For the overseer must be blameless, as God's steward; not self-pleasing, not easily angered, not given to wine, not violent, not greedy for dishonest gain; but given to hospitality, a lover of good, sober minded, fair, holy, self-controlled, holding to the faithful word which is according to the teaching, that he may be able to exhort in the sound doctrine, and to convict those who contradict him.

For there are also many unruly men, vain talkers and deceivers, especially those of the circumcision, whose mouths must be stopped: men who overthrow whole houses, teaching things which they ought not, for dishonest gain's sake. One of them, a prophet of their own, said,

"Cretans are always liars, evil beasts, and idle gluttons." This testimony is true. For this cause, reprove them sharply, that they may be sound in the faith, not paying attention to Jewish fables and commandments of men who turn away from the truth. To the pure, all things are pure; but to those who are defiled and unbelieving, nothing is pure; but both their mind and their conscience are defiled. They profess that they know God, but by their deeds they deny him, being abominable, disobedient, and unfit for any good work.

But say the things which fit sound doctrine, that older men should be temperate, sensible, sober minded, sound in faith, in love, and in perseverance: and that older women likewise be reverent in behavior, not slanderers nor enslaved to much wine, teachers of that which is good, that they may train the young wives to love their husbands, to love their children, to be sober minded, chaste, workers at home, kind, being in subjection to their own husbands, that God's word may not be blasphemed. Likewise, exhort the younger men to be sober minded. In all things show yourself an example of good works. In your teaching, show integrity, seriousness, incorruptibility, and soundness of speech that can't be condemned, that he who opposes you may be ashamed, having no evil thing to say about us. Exhort servants to be in subjection to their own masters and to be well-pleasing in all things, not contradicting, not stealing, but showing all good fidelity, that they may adorn the doctrine of God, our Savior, in all things.

Chapter 1: 1-16

2. Group brackets together that cover a main idea or topic. Grab the Bible translation you plan to use for your study and compare your sections. Write the corresponding chapter and verse numbers along your bracketed margin.

3. Circle key words or underline main ideas on your subsequent readings, focusing on big picture items.

Cut these out as bookmarks to help mark your place in your reading and your journal.

Prepare

- Who is the author and audience?
- What do you know about them?
- Where are they?
- What are the key features of their location?
- When was this written?
- When did the events take place?
- What is the genre?

Divide

- Place brackets in the margins where a main idea starts and stops.
- Clues include change in subject, location, tone, characters, etc.
- Group together verses and paragraphs that cover one BIG idea, sigular event, or theological concept.

LIFE

- Let the original author speak to the original audience.
- Investigate words and sentences within their paragraphs.
- Fill in the gaps from outside sources.
- Explore the bigger picture and similiar passages.

LIVE

- Let the lesson linger.
- Invite in community.
- Voice the TRUTH.
- Enter into worship!

Revealed
BIBLE STUDY METHOD

revealedbiblestudy.com

Made in the USA
Columbia, SC
12 November 2024